Pra

The Sins of

"A certain grief is exposed in *The Sins of Sweet Mortality;* Marilyn Fox and Nancye McCrary expose the broad brush strokes of humanity with the deep blues of living. From San Francisco to a walnut grove, the artists take us places, transport us with saturation of color and the music of intentionally well-placed sounds. In tandem, Fox and McCrary have created a deeply felt sphere of art, emotion, and place."

—ERICA ANDERSON-SENTER, AUTHOR OF
MIDWESTERN POET'S INCOMPLETE GUIDE TO SYMBOLISM

"McCrary's paintings and Fox's poetry dance together like the generative rhythm of the breath. The visual and linguistic choreography of their creation—the cyclical inhale and exhale—deeply connect and enliven the senses."

—JESSICA SHARPENSTEIN, MINDFULNESS ARTS EDUCATOR

"In *The Sins of Sweet Mortality,* paintings and poetry intersect, one form of art speaking to the other. Fox's poems consider the lows and highs of her existence. McCrary's paintings, sometimes haunting, sometimes joyous, always extend the rich imagery of the poetry, drawing the reader into the art of both media."

—SYLVIA WOODS, AUTHOR OF *WHAT WE TAKE WITH US*

"Nancye McCrary's vision is clear, concise and bold. Having her art juxtaposed with Marilyn Fox's poetry lends much joy to the entire book."

—APRIL BERGER, VISUAL ARTIST

"*The Sins of Sweet Mortality* is a courageous journey through layers of grief's anguish and rage, past the agony and ecstasy of love lost and found, and finally falling into the wisdom and peace of nature's arms. This collaboration of paint and poetry pays fierce attention to detail, displaying devotion to artistic excellence and authenticity. Rich with powerful content and color, this book will beckon the reader to return to its pages like visiting an old friend."

—SUE MASSEK, RECIPIENT OF THE KENTUCKY GOVERNOR'S FOLK HERITAGE AWARD

the Sins of
Sweet Mortality

AN ARTISTIC CONFLUENCE

Marilyn Fox & Nancye McCrary

The Sins of Sweet Mortality
AN ARTISTIC CONFLUENCE

Marilyn Fox & Nancye McCrary

ISBN   978-1-958094-09-9

BOOK & COVER DESIGN 🐾 EK LARKEN

Ron Perrin, Art House Obscura 🐾 Photos
Sharon Ruble 🐾 Photos
Eye Scout Images 🐾 Photos

For more information about these paintings
and other artworks by Nancye McCrary, visit www.mccrarystudio.com.

EastOver Press encourages the use of our publications in educational settings.
For questions about educational discounts, contact us online:.
www.EastOverPress.com *or* info@EastOverPress.com

PUBLISHED IN THE UNITED STATES OF AMERICA BY

EASTOVER
— PRESS —

ROCHESTER, MASSACHUSETTS
WWW.EASTOVERPRESS.COM

For all the poets and painters, seen and unseen,
who make their art in times of joy and times of sorrow
in secluded hours and stolen moments ...

for those who support us,
who acknowledge our need to make sense
of this crazy world where everything seems connected
but nothing adds up ...

and with love, our only lodestar ...

we are your sisters.

Contents

A Few Words from the Artists

We are rural lesbians who independently chose to move from large urban areas (Marilyn from Chicago, Nancye from San Francisco) to a place largely unknown. Both of us live on many acres with abundant wildlife, which is frequently apparent in our work. Both of us have earned terminal degrees (Marilyn, Ph.D. in Literature; Nancye, Ed.D. in Instructional Systems Design), and both of us are now retired from our "day jobs."

In what follows, we offer the reader a glimpse into our lives and our friendship. In *The Sins of Sweet Mortality* we combine poetry and painting, juxtapose voice, image, and sensation, in an attempt to create a multi-layered collection that we hope readers will view as rich, textured, and full of possibility.

NANCYE: For me, Marilyn's poetry is all about sensory experience, created with intelligence that stirs the mind and depths that reach into the soul. I relate to that in quite visceral ways.

MARILYN: And in my mind, Nancye's paintings, particularly her use of color, awaken a hunger in the heart, a thirst for a kind of divine beauty. Her paintings silently remind us to *see*. These images offer color and visual pattern that I believe deepens the poetic experience.

NANCYE: These poems "paint" vivid images, too, which is what drew me to them. We agreed from the outset that the paintings are intended to *illuminate* the poems rather than *illustrate* content.

Marilyn. Agreed. That's one important intent of our collaboration. We were already fans of each other's independent art, and—particularly as a result of this project—we both have been inspired in our respective art forms as we continue to experience and react to each other's ongoing work.

Nancye: Exactly right. Some of my paintings are specifically driven by Marilyn's poems, others came to life in conversation with the poet, and still others had been created even before we started this journey.

Marilyn. That's true of my writing, as well. The utter beauty of this whole project is that we've come together as collaborators from notably different backgrounds. But we share aesthetic sensibilities.

Nancye: While I've been drawing and painting for most of my life, exhibiting work in group and solo exhibits in numerous places, I have also been an art teacher, professor of art and education, and director of a program for struggling adolescents. Teaching comes easy for me and has rewarded me with a sense of accomplishment and contribution. Teaching has sustained me, yet my passion for painting has persisted throughout my life. I followed a desire to help troubled youth, found educational research rewarding, but until now, I never found the means to focus on painting, to find my way toward deeper expression through visual art.

Marilyn. Like Nancye, I've been producing art for more than fifty years, and like Nancye, I felt the pressures of making a living. I, too, loved teaching and writing, and was briefly an academic. But I opted for another path: medical publishing, which allowed me to combine my academic interests and make a living. And yet, I always wrote—first poetry, then a novel, then back to poetry—during the time I was in school and throughout my publishing career.

Admittedly, my career was satisfying; I'm proud of what I've accomplished, having come from a small exurban town, a grandchild of immigrants, and the first in my family to earn a college degree. And yet it wasn't enough. I had to write, to lose myself in a line of words, their "sound and sense," the surprise at what lay beneath the surface, what lived in my subconscious. The poems in this volume are organized according to the periods in which they were created. That's why a reader might notice style shifts from section to section. I find joy in a "well-wrought urn" that is a poem. And through my writing, I make peace with the guilt and grief that comes from being human.

NANCYE: Some of my most powerful teaching experiences have been collaborative, where two or more teachers work together to plan, design, and deliver instruction. So, when I began to read Marilyn's poetry, it occurred to me that we might learn from working together, take on the challenge of combining poetry and painting, joining the poetic and the visual aesthetic, and working together to create something greater than the singular poetic or the singular visual by combining our aesthetic approaches. In this book, we work together—not to ornament each other's work, but to explore an aesthetic partnership, a convergence born from a dialogue that both celebrates our similarities and embraces our differences.

As we talked about this project, becoming more excited with each conversation and the real possibility of sharing with others our art and what it means to be an artist, we realized we had crucial questions to answer:
- *How can a painting respond to a poem without being illustrative?*
- *How might poetry and painting enhance or illuminate each other?*
- *How can we achieve what Plutarch said of these two art forms: "painting is silent poetry, and poetry is painting that speaks"?*

And so we began to dig deeper into the unique qualities of poetry and painting. Both art forms have long histories of communicating that which cannot easily be told. in common language. Both aim far beyond what educational theorist Maxine Greene called *the anesthesia of daily human activity*. Both reach for a kind of wide-awakeness.

As the poet Wallace Stevens said, because poetry and painting operate at the intersection of imagination and reality, these arts assume a prophetic stature and become a "vital assertion of self."[*]

In this book we explore such assertions of self with an eye toward creating a novel convergence of our respective works, merging them together like two separate rivers at their confluence to create something new from wholly different sources. In so doing, we learned how the flow of such joining, mixing, and mingling can enhance the reading and viewing experience while maintaining the friction of unique origination and creative independence.

Our intent is to awaken the observer toward imagining what may not be immediately obvious in either language or image. Both elements—the visual and the literary—are layered like a palimpsest, inviting you to uncover other worlds. We hope you will enjoy the flow.

[*] (*Relations Between Poetry and Painting*, Metropolitan Museum of Art lecture, 1951)

First

14

The Swimmer

He stands alone
One hand shading his eyes
Surveying the water below.

Moving slowly down the bank
His body a brown smoothness
Winding on the path between the weeds
He smells the mud and mulberry
Mingling with the willows. Smiles.

He had lain with a woman the night before
But she lacked what he needed most
The sweetness of freedom
That indomitable rhythmic will.

Pushing into the water slowly
He gives himself up to the chill
Bittersweet nature
The monotonous rock of the waves.

Fish-like he slices the water
Slips with half a splash in the sun
Pulling his body with long-armed strokes
Through the ribbons of river around him.

Arching his broad brown back
In a rhythmic heave and slide
He strikes for the steeple clock
A good quarter mile across.

Time drowns in the slice and heave
Only the river survives
Beating a fierce tattoo on his pulses
Keeping the swimmer alive.

The Wedding Ring

She was a queen of possibility
At thirty-three a dream waiting to come true
Dressed in blue-white tulle
Trimmed lace designed to frame
The angled planes of her expectant face.

He was muscled grace
Grown much alone in the cold bright sun of circumstance
That moved him honestly to love the way she danced
Like summer clouds drifting through a half moon sky.

Yet his tanned face flickering a smile
Traced just a hint of hesitation
As he paced the slow line
Suspended time
Before he took her slim gold ring of confirmation
As a homeless boy might take a fire-banked coal
Half heedful of the white-hot heart within.

A Street Going Nowhere

A street going nowhere
Gathering all roads to itself
Holding the lives of people
Continually known knowing me
As I never was then
And am not even now.

And time just the light at the corner
Not far from my house continues
Making from silhouettes reeling and bending
In the frenzy of child's play
Ghosts dancing wild pirouettes
In homage to death.

And easier to write of eternity glibly
So much metaphysical laundry strung out neatly on lines
Than to tell what I know of the old man
In the empty garden of his last year
Cursing goddamnit that bitch of a spring
Coming late in its ignorant stubbornness.

Or the sound of a dove
In the morning summer days
Of my growing up years
Filtered through shadows of third street
Going nowhere
Gathering all roads to itself.

The Gardener

Old George's
Gardened again
Grafted terra firma
Feeling the ground
His way around
Not easy these days for George.

But his garden grows
Without the bells or cockle shells
And proverbial earthly delights
No St. George here no spear
No shield just stakes
And rags and tags.

No myths
Mud no blood
No snakes to spear
Here.
Just old Georgie
Growing toward death.

Still-life: 1973

Still at just the meeting place
Of time and space
The sour smell of sweat on a sick bed
The old man discovered dead at noon
No one of us knew how long.
The raging gone days before
The crying done alone at night
The mouth's stain still on the wall.

Where are you now
Sweet father dear?
There where the gray corpse lay
Hunched up hollow-cheeked
The last breath sucked to the gut?
And are you still sweet father?
And are you still?

Or does the mind in time transform
The stinking sweat and spittle
Make of brittle bones and sallow skin
Magnificent daddy again?
Or are you still
At just the meeting place
Of time and space?

The Moon is Black

The Moon is Black

She disappeared without a word one day
Like wind-lifted thin smoke scudding silently
From a shallow self-consuming fire inside her head
Too faint to trace even a half-life of carbon blue sound
Against the rain smudged moon.

We found her tied in soft gauze cloth
Like bleached birch branches
Draped and propped poor sticks and shocks
Shaking small seeds of sense
Against her smooth dry skull
Rattling faintly like an uncollected gourd
Gone off the snow-blown fence.

She weathered weeks of winter
Biting on her tattered frame
Picked clean by the lean eager crows in her brain
Until only a small thin kite of her will remained
To catch the strength of March at Equinox.

Flared sun hung high
Flung vectors of light lining the sky in all directions
Drenching up the old sweet nag of Spring
Sprung
Flame blown
The moon is hung with rain at noon.

And now she lullabies to me in dreams
Not once but many times
Her voice like measured chimes deepened by rain
Carries mournful steady rings and rings
 and rings my name
Far down within the hollowed ear of sound she sings
The dark thick blood back in the moon
Brings it high and full against the blank June sky.

A Small Stroke of Luck

On a fine bright Sunday in June
As the blue breeze brushed the deep green trees
God poked his hairy fingers through my mother's eyes
The tangled tissue of her brain collapsing like a
Gossamer web yielding to rain.
For a small slow string of time
Filaments floated aimlessly across her mind's sky
She blinked blanks
She cried.

When she tried to speak
A weak babble of sounds sprayed the air
Like the stuttered hiss and lisp
Of a far-off muddy brook broken by rocks.

She was dazed
Crazed in the clear light.
I pulled her close
My lips grazing her slack cheek.
"Speak, Mother, speak."
I cried into her glazed eyes
Spied one bloodied spider of thought
Spinning patches from her torn belly
Mending tears. Tears ended
My mother made my name.
I prayed.

Christmas Ride

My mother likes to be taken about
Shuttled in and out of deserted streets
Like a quiet blue thread in a tapestry
Where our lives are laid out in relief.

My mother is getting her Christmas ride
Down to the river and up to the school
We weave through the winter brown town of her life
Its colors bleached out by the light.

I lie to my mother as we make the return
Up through the ice-patched strangers' street
To the looming Home on Baptist Hill
Its golden bricks flowered in holiday firs.

My mother cries as I wheel her about
Through corridors strewn with broken souls
Their eyes on wires tongues on fire
A primary prism of white desire
For the winter brown town of their dreams.

Hands

Empty hands fluttering in the hot air
Her mouth a stutter of confusion
I imagine her settling in
While I run in the snow alone.

I remember our last visit
My strong hands tendering care
Pulling and wiping the small broken body
A slow quiet agony of pain and will
Suffering my mouth to kiss her lonely cheek
As I would kiss a child I loved
As she kissed me.

And for a brief time
I lay my head in her thin lap
While she stroked my heavy hair
Telling me with steady hands
I could love her still
As she loved me
Her childless child
Running in the snow
Alone.

The Willow Trees

I like to think
My mother's back
Behind the willow trees
Among her lost children
And half remembered dreams.

The air is more than air there
Sweet against the skin and strong
Enough to hold her quiet stare of resignation
In a fine suspension
Like the deep blank eyes
Of a mourning dove
Hung
Between the leaves
At dawn.

I like to think
She knows me when I move up close
To frame my hands
Around her fragile (almost wild) expression.

But no.
I see
The flash of recognition
Crushed
Behind the two black holes
Of her eyes
Collapsing
Back to stardust.

My Mother is Small Now

My mother is small now
Bent low and scraped out from inside.

What lives is close to the surface
Mottled skin stretched tight
Over the bleeding bone.

She knows me
Barely
Past a stumble of gnarled neurons
Clumped in slagged heaps.

She is weak
An old sick animal who might be shot
Or left to die at dusk
In the fringe of woods
Edging a circle of huts.

But we keep her
With us
Who came from her
Great smooth belly
Toothless and dumb
Drugged on life.

Your Dying Dives Me Deeper into Song

To find that place where truth
Ingrained in shells of sound
Forms smooth wise pearls of consolation
To clench against my harrowed heart
For strength.

But alabaster rose
wants grief to grow
beneath the reef
amid the weedy incandescence.

Mother, I Put On Your Rings

Mother I put on your things
I bring the chair around your bed.

I dread the frightened rhythm
Rocking in your shallow chest
Yet press my hand for comfort there.

I kiss the graceful hollow place
Where death is being carved from innocence
By moonlight curving downward
As it flings itself in rings
To limn your face on mine.

Mother I can brace myself.
Mother I can hold my breath
For no more breath
The space of death the nowhere
Where you want to go
The no.

But no I cannot go
With rings
I cannot go with all your things
With you in me
Still holding on
For dear life.

Mother, You Fooled Me

Your dying was so slow
I thought you'd never go.
But you slipped away
Like thin smoke in a gray sky
No goodbye, just died.

I Am All Unmothered

Unmothering child
With nothing to show for this mother
Who made me
But words
Flat like the pictures of children
Not children
Not blood from my blood bleeding
But black
Not beyond my control
But controlled
Not the sign of my body extended
The symbol
The line without point

Mother, You Are Not That Stone

That fine granite death
Pressing the sun-swelled grass
Grown thick and blue on a hill
You do not own, you do not know
That name-surrounded lake
Where small brown ducks
Pluck bloody tufts of order
From their bony breasts
And all is rest.
The rest is gone.
The dawn-wrecked moon and you
Are nowhere there
The air is still
Along the hill
You do not own
The stone.

My Mother Lived in a State of Grace

Gone wild.
Weeds grown to wall the garden of her mind
Tangled
Thoughts grown thick to choke her speech
With halt and moan.
She blessed me
In a state of grace
Gone wild.

If Paul Gauguin

Returning again and again returning
To a brown face on a blank wall
I am convinced that Paul Gauguin
Hid spring beneath an autumn branch
And willed it rose when he returned from France.

So I'm looking hard here
Among the hushed tones
Behind the crushed hibiscus
For some trace of your face.

I can just make out the hill
See the rime along the edges of your name
Where the deep-dug grave of small proportion
Squares a blue circled ache in my brain.

I can even hear the old refrain
From Psalms past singing
Glimpse palimpsests of snowy angels
Stunned to faded adumbrations
Tumbling on the dead white moon.

So why if Paul Gauguin
Can will the branches rose
And stain the deep ground carmine
Can't I erase the gray metallic resting place
That hides your face?

Chinatown

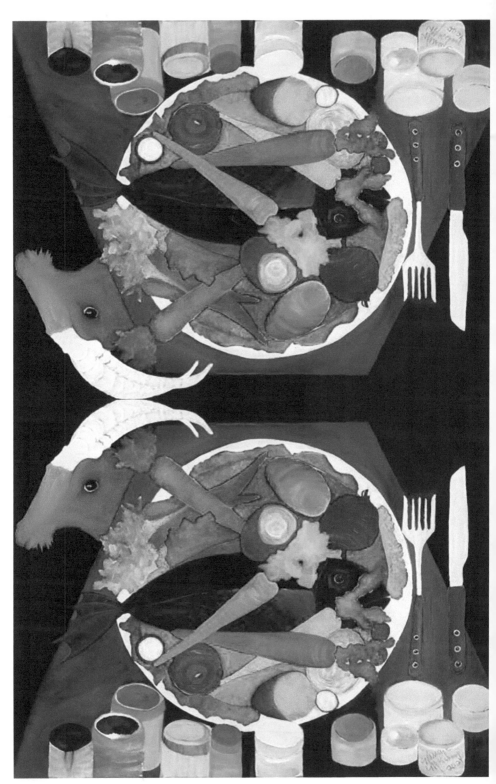

38

Chinatown

I'm no longer young
And well-traveled enough
To take the streets where I find them
And where they find me.

The women here speak in high round sounds
That drop like lead to the ground
When the men come around
Smelling faintly still of decay
And the withered blossoms of old ceremony
Staggering daughters.

They sell me a crazed white dish
Blue fish bright eye
Splashed on somewhere near Xían
By a woman whose wide brush
Must have hooked the sky
Who must have mothered one too many daughters
In the hungry countryside.

I eat small bits of flesh
Mixed with rice and roots
And a poem fans out like a peacock tail
Torn iridescence
On the shaded walk in Budapest:

"I am near forty and look it
dragged down by the niceness of paper
thumbs raw brain blunt
from the paging of it.

I am older than years counting.
I am back behind my mothers
Asleep in a nest of rounded boxes
That drop from me secretly one by one

Born in thin sheets of black and white mystery
The cry in the goat's pen behind the pavilion
The mangled foot
Dead daughter in the well."

San Francisco

San Francisco is rich with the homeless
Legions of ventured entrepreneurs
Own small parts of the streets' dark grottos
Or lease the sidewalks with their brokered hearts
Signing time-share agreements
Sometimes in blood.
They sell god or sex
Or the certain sin or either
Tongue the air with their truths
They stare. They roll and weave a fine line
Dance for a nickel
Dime you to death.

No trust in the government
They put all their money in the Hibernia Bank
Guarding the fine glass doors
With their mortgaged careers
Maimed and cut
Vigilantes lamed
For a dollar's worth of space
At seven percent.

I am compelled by their subliminal selves
Buying from these ragged capitalists
On the margins of their lives
A sure thing
And get for my investment
This return. They fix on me
The bright blue eye of fear.

Between High Point and Saint Paul

On the road between High Point and Saint Paul
Just where the stand of stubbled corn
Beards the slow gray November hill
My lover speaks aloud to me
Psychologist's truths.
They are perfectly red and round
Like the circled mouths of Greek women
Coming on to the god in the hill
Shaping the sharp logic of ecstasy
With their hollowed tongues.

And all the while my lover speaks
I hear my mother's whispered cry
To stroke beneath her ear
Where smooth blue skin begins
To cover a round collar of bone.

And all the while my lover speaks and my mother cries.
I drive, caught by the eyes of an animal
Just at the crest of the hill
Where the needled eye of god is small
Hard threading
Between High Point and Saint Paul.

New Orleans Washboard Girl

Hey, washboard girl
Sweet smoky blue musician
Tattered strummer in the street
Girl, you
With thimbled thumbs rubbed smooth
Across the grooves,
Are you some god called saint
From heaven come
To wail my sins away?

Or are you more
At prayer
A servant sent
From some indentured part of hell
To sell your songs for passage
To the promised land?

Occasional Light Chop

I am sitting here in occasional light chop
Thirty-eight thousand feet above my problems.
I understand from Newton
This can't go on forever
But Einstein said
It's better than it might have been.

So I sit back, relax
Pick a point in Neverland
Grin and bear the fine green line
Between the plane and heaven.

They say:
"God knows
Just exactly where we are at all times."
I don't believe it for a minute.

Airplane Ride

I am pinned between two men
Riding (as I have for centuries)
In silence.

They are kind
Helping me off with my coat
Smiling at the lines around my eyes
Politely eying my swollen breasts
Heavy hung against my great taut belly.

I am displayed in a sealed case
Seated like a Maya figurine
Chipped at the corners
Terra cotta legs spread out. Crying.
My large rough hands pressed hard on the world they
made inside me squeezing out daughters and sons.

I am caught behind my naked eyes
By the large boy
Breaking over me in rough waves
Scalding my skin.

I am not yet nine
And dry sand already
Blowing down to the river
Dissolving out to the sea.

I am not kind.
Inside
I am a cramped fiend
Grainy pieces of my soul
Smashed back together
By deep forces at the ocean's floor.

I am a thin shell
Delicate
Silica smooth and polished

Resurfacing to dry in the high thin air
Where they blow their breath on me softly
As they sleep.

Beyond the Road to Delavan

In a gone grazed field
Beyond the road to Delavan
An old one scarved and shawled for winter
Stooped and heavy hung with time
Winds her flock of dams and wethers
Snagged in thick-spun knots
Around and round the deep wooled rams
Her crooked staff stumps the clodded ground
Until they loom themselves in pairs
Before the shuttled comb of god
Who weaves the wolf's head
Brave and hungry
Draws the body lean and gray
Slams the door down hard to heaven
Carries them away.
The bitten branch with woolen hangs
Beyond the road to Delavan
Where no farm stands and no one herds
Beneath a bitter almond sky.

Melancholy
Savage

A Sometime Sappho Answered

Cunning Lingo?
For a girl like you?
Impossible.
Your mouth's gone slack
Too many idle conversations
Across the heavy linen
While the sun slants itself to oblivion.

I am made in the silent light
Of a naked morning sun
Not in the curtained comfort of an alehouse evening
With a cocktail in your hand.

Melancholy Savage

I am fierce.
I should be wrapped around with skins
Stone scraped and dried against the bone-bright sky,
A melancholy savage
Soaked in birch smoke
Smeared with ash
Beneath the eye scar gashed
Washed with want for the woods
Where a woman sits in a tree
Tearing tangles from her hair
Teeth bright
Tongue sweet with sex
Just beyond my reach.

Mermaid

I love a woman who touches
Touching to me in the sea
Her murmur on my lips and breasts
Subtle rising
Sudden fall
Across my arching back.

I have visions of a lifetime
With such a woman's hands upon me.
Cresting, falling in the sea
Beneath the weave of evensong
Sweet murmuring to me.

I would have these visions
This woman rocking gently
In the light beneath the sea
My hands and mouth discovering
Hidden places in the weave
Comes murmuring and shuddering
Arching under me.

Jane Eyre at the Beach

If I take Jane to the beach with me
What shall I do?
Can I be true to Jane and you?

Jane is good and fair
And quite completely there
From start to end
Just where and when I want her.
Sweet blue anemone
Pressed between the angled pages by the sea.

But when you come
Like some deep driven rose
Rising full bloom from the glistened reef
A rendezvous of ebony and gold
Jane fades, grows old
Bores me.

Water Dreams

From my sprawl on the smooth muscle of rock
I watch you
Waist deep in a sun catch of water
Near the shore of this indigo bay
Opened out to the untended sea.

You are wild but still
Quite civilized
Poised
A woman waiting
On the edge of your dream.

The Curve of Linearity

Donne says
"We are a little world made cunningly."
I see indeed almost precisely what he means:
You are the universe to me
The curve of linearity
Brown stars speckling skin
Spread thin across the milky sky of your unfolding body
Brave organ of all breathing.

Nova

You are pure flame flared
The fierce force of a star streak
Stunning the pitch cold sky.

And I am love's dark fool
Mad for light from the bright candle
Of your adventure with the world.

So I come
Bare flesh and bones
Heart naked
Wanting to be burned.

Subliminal Darkness of Being

If you should ask me
Why I love you,
I would say:
You are subliminal darkness of being,
A black rose growing just beyond imagining
Beyond the touch of ordinary light
Beyond the orderly dimension of reflection.

The Dark Coil

The dark coil of the sun of your being
Bends me into the deep hot thrill of you
Like some half-crazed cold moon
Spun loose from a dying star
Spun close to the flush of life again
I arc and spin
Blazed dancer in the charged sky.

Some Forms of Love

Some forms of love are marked by time
Like the circled lines of a great tree
Heart ringed precisely hard
Held from the root to the bark.

But ours forms and reforms itself
Like an island sea on hot sand
The wave and the particle
Passed through the arc of the moon
Bending the darkened shoreline
Curving light from the stars
Struck in the void
Where nothing is all.

Dream

Hey, that lady she's a dream
High and dark
More than seem
She is
Fire and ice
Nice.

That lady is no cloud
In my sky
Fine sun
Wine
That lady
She's mine.

Hey, that lady's gone
Smacked me in the head
Cracked my love
Killed it dead.

That dream that was
She was
A dream
Gone.

Tongues of Fire

I am a barrier island
Tide wept
Wind shaped
Shoved up with grief
Grudged from a deep rock beneath the reef
Cleaved heart heaved
Hungry for a piece of whole
Of one again.

So if you come to me
When evening washes hesitation from the sky
To lie long and deep against the wind-ribbed dunes
Where doubt's dry shadow disappears
Along the rain light kissing ridge,

You better bridge your way on tongues of fire
Or the ever-drawn suck of my moon-kept sea
Will pluck desire's new shallow roots
Like blue anemones
Torn in the dawn storm.

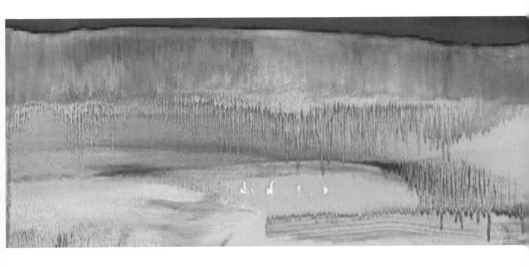

Bête Noire (Again)

This time
I've built an abattoir
Inside my brain
A wild and grisly place
Where I can face the beast in me
And grin.

Bete noir I am
Bete noir again
I wear a shirt of hair
Rough spun with sin
And smile at my reflection dimly glimpsed
Inside the splattered glass.

It's cold in here
But isn't it just what I want
To seal the bleeding parts?
Congeal my heart?

I think it just might be
Hell's not so bad
Not what they say
More vague
An almost empty sky
Tinged orange around the dusky fringes of horizon
As though a fire were taking place
Some miles away
Without a trace of heat.

Logic's Love is Light

Like summer shades
Pink and blue carnations
Colored quite correctly
From their right grown roots
To perfect petalled stems.

But mine is dark
Deep purple veined
Blood wine vermillion
Sucking sweet black earth
To make herself magnificent
In the crush of fallen sun.

Diana Divesting Herself

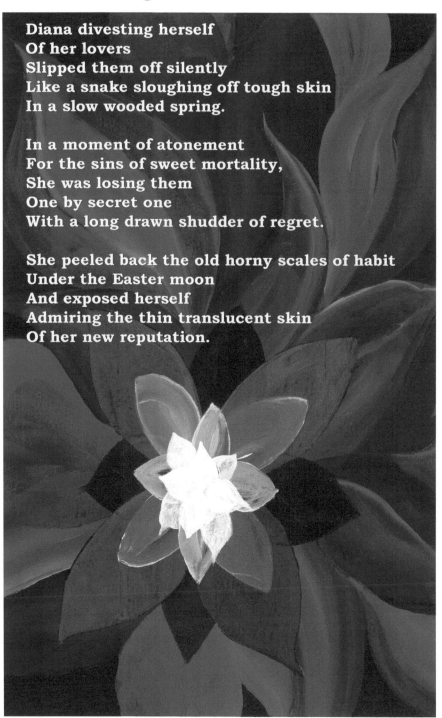

Diana divesting herself
Of her lovers
Slipped them off silently
Like a snake sloughing off tough skin
In a slow wooded spring.

In a moment of atonement
For the sins of sweet mortality,
She was losing them
One by secret one
With a long drawn shudder of regret.

She peeled back the old horny scales of habit
Under the Easter moon
And exposed herself
Admiring the thin translucent skin
Of her new reputation.

I(mage)

The fluttered lash
The half closed lid
The flush the crush
Comes all over me
The rush
The spring in fall
Behind the rain
Blown circles of rose rising with the sun
The crest
The ground-grown swell upheaving
Beneath bittersweet sedge
You in the terraced garden
Pulling poems from boxwoods.

I Love Your Power

In the evening, with music
You take the questions of my heart
And like a skilled musician
Make them disappear behind your eyes.

You hold my wild soul softly
In your cupped hands
As a keeper of birds
Calms the mourning dove.

Oak Park Nocturnes

Lucifer

I'm stuck
Like that frickin' pretty Satan
In an ice ball.

At least he did something
Started a new religion
Knew it wasn't enough to cry over the dead
And then go home.

No, it was more complicated:
Choices
Formality
Getting and begetting
Fighting over a twig and a plum
That's the real beginning.

So back to me.
Stuck.
Trying to write.
Construct.
My father died
My mother died
I didn't have kids
So it's just me
Wandering around in the desert
Looking for Lucifer.

Angel

She had the look of a woman who'd been saved
One too many times.
You know, that beatific smile and furtive glance
That said Jesus had been messin' with her.

Angel was her given name
(I kid you not)
But she screwed every guy in sight
Then went to church on Sunday.

I was curious
Used to spy on her in the alley
Watch as she sat on the porch smokin'
Lookin' around for Jesus.

He must have come for her,
Finally,
Because her brother sold the house
And threw the *Watch Towers* in the trash.

Laurie

Married a doctor
Had three daughters and a son they imported from
Romania
Moved to a big house on Kenilworth
Got feminized
Flirted with every girl who came her way
Including yours truly.

It was a painful thing
Watching myself get torn to pieces
By a straight girl
An experiment, no less, in how to leave your husband

Which she did.
Married a man who played the guitar.
That was the eighties
At least in my neighborhood.

Kevin

Married late
A woman from Kansas
Hauled her and her Pier-1 furniture
All the way back to Chicago.

He got them a place on Halstead Street
But she was allergic to noise
So they ended up on Division
In the heart of old Oak Park.

His father was ecstatic.
Finally.
Bought a big wedding and a trip to St. Croix
Sat back to wait for the kids.

But the whole thing ended badly.
Too many thorny issues.
Not the one he expected.
Too many calls from Boys Town.

John

He knew all the conversions
John did.
A true alcoholic
Unlike the rest of us who just drank too much.

In the late afternoons on a park bench
Up by the Frank Lloyd Wrights
He stared at his past and future.
Slipped the flask to his lips.
Sighed.
Sipped.
Smiled.
It was sunny and cool.
Time arrested.
Away.

He was always there as I drove home
And again in the morning light
Drinking in reality
Disappearing inside his coat
About to escape.

The Bent-Over Man

Walking fast toward the intersection
Arms swinging like pendulums
Stops on a dime at the intersection
His body Jack-knifed like a swimmer
Arms back and up, head jutted out
Ready to plunge when the light turns green.

How does he breathe?
How can he see the sky?
Can no physician help this man?
No Reiki master make him straight?

He catches me staring,
Casts back a hateful glance.
Ashamed at my stupidity, I look away.
Pity should be doled out sparingly.

Syrian Man

Beats a staccato tattoo on the tabletop
Slender fingers inching toward the Marlboros
Fidgeting in the chair. Figuring.
His American wife gone
To the spa or god knows where
With a squeeze of his shoulder she left.
"Back in a few."

Indifferent to me
Covetous
Fingering the scarves
Smelling the soaps
Fingertips playing the filigreed gaming boards
Backgammon, chess, and all the rest
Made by his friends in Homs.

I catch myself in his mirror
Feigning indifference as I examine the prices
But needing to own these things
As though by having them I get a piece of him,
of that thousands-year-old past.

He knows.
"Nice, lady, very nice.
But price remains the same."
He left then, left me with all of it.
Went out to smoke and never returned.
At least that's what I heard.

Gertrude

Sets up shop on the Ides
Near the corner of Van Buren and Oak Park
Reads her poetry.

I've heard it before and only half-listen
Checking her out instead:
Same outfit
Same make-up
Everything the same.
A gnome
Jaw too heavy
Nose too wide and full at the tip.

I smile at her plainness
Bored by her predictability.
Smug (I could write and I was pretty;)
Reflective (of course I wasn't writing now.)

This time something was different:
People stopped to listen
Gathered and bent into each other
Murmured something about the voice.
Embarrassed voyeurs
Moved sideways to where she stood,
Crammed cash in the jar.
Hurried off
Transfixed.

A Lady Needs a Dream

I used to watch her at the Berwyn Bar and Grill
Fidgeting
Long legs curled around the bar stool
Stabbing at the notebook with her pencil
Like a bird grabbing an insect
Devouring all the items on her list
Marking progress
Making time for one more thing
Always behind
Hungry
Hopes pinned on pretend
Her mind moving faster than the earth moves
Imperceptible.
Still.
A lady needs a dream.
Even here.

Cheap Thrills

I wanted cheap thrills
The ache between my legs that strangeness brings
And I got everything I wanted.
On and on and on they came
Until they slapped me silly
Is as silly does. It was cheap thrills
For forty days and forty-one-night-stands
In just divide to every year I'd lived
Just so and just that way.
I paid for what I got.
You get just what you pay for.
Not one cheap thrill more.

The Queen of Egypt

When I was the Queen of Egypt
I kept my tomb spare
A bit of gold around the throne
Bare white linens for the wrap
The air sans fragrances
The urns with just one word:
Guts.

Here in the now it's cluttered
The hum and mutterings of devices
Houses filled with bibelots and junk
Ceramic dogs on ribbons
Cats in the corners
Purring their reminders
I'm dead.

Dead Reckoning

I'm Not Made for This Paper

I wasn't born to it,
But the writing follows me
Curves and hollows me even into the horse's shed
Where the withered flanks of an old mare
Shake off death in a curl of steam,
Or down to the heron pond in summer
Where the small round stone of her body drowned
As we went round and round.

There is no reckoning:
Life can end with the shrug of the last leaf
Falling from a dying tree,
Begin in surprise of carnelian shoot
Sprung up in the drought ground of a plowed field.

So I ask for grace through words
For holiness in the heaviness of something
No one knows just what
Exploded in the face of god
For healing in the glistened scar
Gashed down through space
That shows we've been somewhere
We can't remember being.

Small Sounds

Small sounds:
The body breaking down
Joint mice rustling among the bones
The breath a little short.
A tree branch sawing and moaning
In the woods by First Path
Waiting for a strong wind to end it.

All falls down
Because something moved away
Back then
When everything was nothing,
Nowhere to be disturbed,
But was.

Rose the Storm

Before the storm
A great flock of starlings
Peppered the sky
Dropped
All in a shot
Soared
Streaked toward the trees
Disappeared into their chatter.

Rose as a million speckled scolds
Shrieked at the hawk
Slammed by the wind
Fallen into a cauldron of lightning
Scalding rock and branch
As an ocean of rain
swelled in great green plumes
Across the ridge.

Hawks

Two hawks hunting at the edges
Of the highway
A flutter of danger in the outspread wings
Tunnels of air barreling behind the trucks
Sucking them into the road.

A handsaw of hawks
Down
Blown into awkward poses
Bodies torqued and twisted above their prey
Feathers waving in the rush.

I think about saving them somehow
Scooping them up
Blowing the breath back
Lifting their broken wings
Heaving them heavenward
For god to fix.
Praying on them.

Shooting Star

The fish are wide-eyed
Near to drowning,
Their ruffled gills a slow stutter,
Their mouths a grief-work of cold.

The pond is flash-frozen
And the fish work the water
In the one remaining channel.

There are too many fish
Not enough loaves
A miracle is wanted
Here in the too-shallow pond.

There is no miracle.
Ten fish dead at daybreak.

I make the sign of infinity
Go back to the house by the fire.
Dream:
I am gasping for air
Drowning.

A star falls into the pond.
The fish flash their fins.

I Slip Through the Pond

I slip through the pond
Naked but for the paddles and fins.
I am alone.

The adornments of herons and red wings all flown.
The turtles buried in the limey mud.
It's cold.

The willows whip and bend in the wind
As I ascend the ladder
A shiver of muscle glistening and chafed.

I long for the light to stay
But the day slips through me elusive and subtle
Like a small breeze through chimes.

The Surface of the Pond

The surface of the pond is like old glass
Undulating in the September sun.
I long to enter through it.
Devolve. Join the shadowy forms below
Become a rhythm of reflected light
Scattered and dappled on the willows
Turn and slip like a turtle off the branch
Cut like a bass for prey at the bank.
Stay.
My cry as old as that first cry:
A woman standing at the precipice
Made to descend.
A rough hand above the brow
Looking for the way.
Turning back is not an option.

Watching: Easter Morning

Watching
A huge Charolais away from the herd
Looking into the trees
A ghostly guard of some unknown intention
Keeping off by herself.

Running
Hard along the rutted path
Brushing the low-hanging branches of locusts
Their spines tearing at her hide
Dissolving into the still dark woods
A hurry of heaving sides and red swollen udder.

Peering
Out from the trees at the base of the path
Her triangle face hung like a charm
On the bracelet of old limey wall
Falling all a stumble above the creek.

We found her calf the next day
Beautifully formed and dead
Like a carving of pure white soapstone
Melting into the ground
Eyes shut tight
Against the pain of resurrection.

The New Spring

Like a young god risen up
Laughing
A sprig of garlic in his teeth.

That's how I think of Jesus at the resurrection
Smiling at the mourners who couldn't see him
There in the garden waiting for his bride.

She came to him
Breasts honeyed and rubbed with myrrh
Bringing bread and figs to feed his long hunger.

Why must you keep him from these simple pleasures?
He was content to die. Knowing
Those who choose eternity are doomed to live there.

Elegy for Jeffrey

1.

It's too quiet here.
I stop to listen:
Something hovering around the edges
Of the garden;
White cat still in the rhododendron
A tight coil
Waiting.

I go back to weeding
Digging out a dandelion
Its perfect yellow petals bargaining
The brave root like a finger trap:
The longer I dig the harder I pull
The stronger the root becomes.
Defiant.
Snapping. Finally.

2.

He said he liked to rub his hands together.
I wondered why until I tried it.
I do it now to get the dirt off.
Pleasure.
A small thing that reminds me of him
The youngest
At the kitchen table silent
Waiting for a small turn
Needing help with our father
Drunk. In no mood for one more son.

3.

There in the hospital he looked at me
The way he used to look across the table
And said what he must have always thought:
"Sis, the more you try to help
The worse it seems to get."

After he died I saved
Everything in sight:
A clip of his hair, shirt, shoes
Cards (no letters)
An empty pack of tissues
Small insects underfoot
Their wings torn, legs bent or broken
The petals of flowers fallen in the dirt
The ashes he became.

4.

I know now what I hear:
His voice
Spinning the copper blades of our wind ornament
Slicing the air in silence.

The Dead Don't Seek Us

I know the dead don't seek us
They don't need us
Or speak to us
They're completed.

We can't hear the dead or see them.
We're the living.
Uncompleted.

No need to rub my hands across her bed
Smooth the places where she lay
Or press her night clothes to my face.
Her scent lingers in the air
But she's gone and doesn't need me anymore.
She's completed.

And yet
When the sky rouges up at dawn
And what lives is borne by the light to rise again
I think I hear her crying
See her far off
Back behind the trees.

To Hide the Shame of Dying

Is that why they discarded their dead?
Cached them away in a limestone cave
Its mouth a slit to shove the bodies in.

Is that why we buried them
To free ourselves from facing
what we'll never see again?
Be again?

I say lay my bones on a funeral pyre
Pray they burn and blow
Through heady winds to Neverland.

Hold out your arms
Embrace me when I'm gone
Love me with your eyes
Watch the gray sky give way to mauve.

An Ache So Deep

An ache so deep
Sweet and sharp
A cry for more and no more
Like god had shoved an awl
Through my heart to the root.

We are all done in this way
In suck and sex and death.

The stake in the ground of us
Down to our mothers and fathers
Down to the thirsty tongues
Of those gone before us
Down to the last divining
The everlasting shove.

Last

The Lost Years

The lost years
At the bottom of the brain
Stirred up in sleep
A tangle of misplaced names
Faces spliced one upon the other
Fears and passions all jig-sawed together.

Mother shape-shifted into lover
Naked and wild around the eyes
Running from me into rivers
Turning into oceans into ponds.

Lost.
Keys and phone misplaced
In an unnamed city of culs de sac and strangers.
Threats looming in the darkness.
Where to turn?

I'm on Edge

Can't seize another day
Need to let it come to me
Slowly
Like my lover
Coming as the earth does
Quietly and with purpose
Giving over to desire
Need time to have its way with me
Embrace me.

Time's a Wasting

I'm not wasting time.
She's wasting me
Away to nothing.
Just a bit of rag and rage to toss around
When no one else is there.

Picked me up along the way
On her long march to nowhere
Strung me out
Played me like some half-forgotten banjo
She found slouching in the corner.

I wanted her to love me
Keep me beautiful and young
Blow a big breath full of longing
Strong and indestructible into my weary soul.

But no. She left me high and dry
Like a drought-filled creek. Just a trickle left
Where a flash flood used to be.
You see, it's space she really loves,
The zero under the line.

The Barren Aunt

I'm content
Finally. To be defined by other women's children
Rooted in my negativity
An imaginary number beneath the line
Divided out to nothing.
Off the ways trees are
Off in the distance
Soft and dark as an animal's shadow.

I'm content
Now. To wander at the edges of the pond
Among the willow trees
See god in a broken branch divided by the snow
Feel the cold. It chaps and chastens.
The fire of frost igniting my desire?
No.
Pinching my resolve
Tight as a slit of mouth pursed shut
To keep temptation out.

When I Die

If I could only see myself
Along the garden wall
I'd make a bargain with the devil
Or even god himself.

"Let me have just this one thing
And I'll be yours forever."

I imagine god as one enormous light.
The devil velvet darkness crushed.

Which one came first?
Can one be struck without the other?

My Life is Like a Leaping Deer

Spring
Glide
Drop
Disappear
Into the autumn trees
Appear
Transformed
Taut

My Old Stray Dog

Is leading me astray. She meanders and I follow
    into the hollows of the hills.
Into the brown broom sedge and blackberry canes
Into the stifle and prickle
Where the limbs of trees and the limbs of deer are
    strewn about.

My old stray dog, she likes to wander. Sniffs and shuffles.
Scuffles through the oak and hickory leaves
Licks the place coyotes lick. Where mineral works its way
    through clay.
Can't hear my call but smells it. Home. Comes back to me.

Half blind.
That's when we all begin to see
What's beneath our feet.
What's through and through with us.

I Want to Die Walking

I want to die walking
Not powdered and diapered
An addled swaddling in a chair
A thing a m'tug shifted through the hours
By women who call me honey.

My name's not Honey
And I want to die walking.

I want to fall all in a stumble
Through the walnuts
Muttering, then die
Be burned with them rubbed against my skin
Their rich rough redolence
Like the incense and myrrh of a queen.

Oh, who will answer my savage prayer
To keep me there
Already married to the ground where I fell
Staked to the axis of the sun
Glowering in the southern sky?

Who will gather my clothes
And cover me in cedar boughs
Dry and hard like I am?
Who will rub the walnuts on my arms?

Will you who come upon me know
That I cannot be made again
To look like the woman I was
Before it blasted me?

Death comes in a furnace of fire
Explodes the flesh from the bone.

The animals know.
They smell the fire,
Rake the rocks with their claws,
Keening.

About the Poet

Born and raised in Dayton, Kentucky, a small town on the hook of the Ohio River, MARILYN FOX earned a Bachelor of Arts degree in English and a Bachelor of Science degree in Biology from Morehead State University, and a master's degree and PhD in English from the University of Kentucky. After a brief stint teaching literature, Fox opted to pursue a career in medical publishing. She served as publications director for a large medical specialty organization in Chicago for many years before returning to Kentucky in 2012.

Fox has been writing poetry since her early twenties and has had poems published over the years in various journals. Her group of poems called "Melancholy Savage" was published in the Harrington Lesbian Fiction Quarterly.

Her poetry reflects a lifetime of thinking about and living in the world. Educated in literature as well as in science and medicine, Fox uses images from the natural world, anatomy, physics, and daily experience to plumb the depths of guilt, grief, longing, infatuation, and loss.

Fox writes from the deep. Her work is personal in a way that inspires feelings about and reflection on one's own lived experiences.

Since retirement, she has returned to rural Kentucky where she now lives close to the earth.

About the Painter

NANCYE MCCRARY's passion for creating thoughtful compositions using intense color is woven throughout her life and professional careers. An experienced visual art teacher, educated in fine arts and education, as well as Instructional Systems Design, she has exhibited her work throughout the United States. She taught visual art in public and private elementary, middle, and secondary schools, including serving as Arts Director in a development center for children and youth with disabilities. McCrary was also Artist-in-Residence for Learning through Education in the Arts (San Francisco), and Youth in Art and Very Special Arts (Marin County, California). Her students won numerous awards in National Scholastic Arts competitions; some were selected to exhibit at the Tennessee Arts Commission Gallery (Nashville), the de Young Museum in Golden Gate Park and the San Francisco Ballet.

McCrary has taught studio courses, art history, art appreciation, art therapy and art education on the post-secondary level, designing and serving as Program Chair for an Art Education teacher preparation program at a small women's college in Georgia. In Kentucky, she served as Assistant and Associate Professor in fine arts and teacher education at the University of Kentucky and at St. Catharine College, where she served as Chair of Professional Studies.

She lives in central Kentucky, where she maintains a painting and teaching studio nestled on 43 acres.

Acknowledgments

Very special thanks to our EastOver Press lead editor and project manager, Scout, for sharing expertise in publishing, the arts, and all things creative. Scout's editing and design suggestions were always what we needed to move forward with this project. In addition to contributing time and expertise, Scout has been a pleasure to work with, patient when we slowed down and inspiring when we were on a roll.

We greatly appreciate the rest of the EastOver Press team, as well—particularly Dr. Walter Robinson, who green-lit this unorthodox book project, Kelly March's promotional finesse, and EOP poetry editor Denton Loving, who provided valuable advice.

Photographers Ron Perrin, (Art House Obscura, Louisville, Ky.) and Sharon Ruble (Lexington, Ky.), and Eye Scout Images (Willisburg, Ky.) who skillfully reproduced many of the paintings for this book. Without their expertise this book would not have been possible.

Our spouses, Beth Gore and Marsha Wilson, have steadied us throughout this project. We so appreciate their loving support as we worked through this idea of combining poetry and painting while maintaining the integrity of each art form. Beth and Marsha have long supported our need to create and made room for our individualities.

Finally, we are grateful to live in a rural community surrounded by nature's endless beauty and strong, smart women. We are fortunate to live in an area of central Kentucky where three communities of religious women (Dominican Sisters of Peace, Sisters of Charity, and Sisters of Loretto) maintain their Motherhouses; where a relatively large community of lesbians make their homes; and where we work closely with Democratic women to make our voices heard and make good trouble together. We so appreciate all the women living here who continue to teach and inspire us.

Illuminations

CPSIA information can be obtained
at www.ICGtesting.com
Printed in the USA
JSHW051903170423
40460JS00001B/1